MYTHICAL MAN

MYTHICAL MAN

DAVID LY

Palimpsest Press
1171 Eastlawn Ave.
Windsor, Ontario. N8S 3J1
www.palimpsestpress.ca

Book and cover design by Kate Hargreaves (CorusKate Design)
Cover photograph by David Clode via Unsplash
Author photograph by Erin Flegg Photography
Edited by Jim Johnstone

 **Anstruther Books**

Palimpsest Press would like to thank the Canada Council for the Arts,
and the Ontario Arts Council for their support of our publishing
program. We also acknowledge the assistance of the Government of
Ontario through the Ontario Book Publishing Tax Credit.

 Canada Council Conseil des Arts
for the Arts du Canada  ONTARIO ARTS COUNCIL
CONSEIL DES ARTS DE L'ONTARIO Ontario

Library and Archives Canada Cataloguing in Publication

Title: Mythical man / David Ly.

Names: Ly, David, author.

Description: Poems.

Identifiers: Canadiana (print) 20200172646 | Canadiana (ebook)
20200172654 | ISBN 9781989287354 (softcover) |
ISBN 9781989287361 (EPUB) | ISBN 9781989287378 (Kindle) |
ISBN 9781989287385 (PDF)

Classification: LCC PS8623.Y3 M9 2020 | DDC C811/.6—dc23

PRINTED AND BOUND IN CANADA

CONTENTS

1.
NOD
AND
BE
POLITE

MYTHICAL MAN (I)

The twist of stray hairs into place,
the twist
of a hairspray lid. Spritz. Freeze
the enviable silhouette.
There, viper scales
frame
a smoky-eyed stare—
you never know where the gaze
will strike.
White peacock feathers weaved
into a black updo,
a taxidermic bird-of-paradise
perched atop, talons
curved to pluck
out admiring eyes.
Enveloped in a bodice constructed
from the exoskeletons
of Hercules beetles,
lacquered shells
that catch the light
in every pose,
he flows down
a clinical runway
in a silver taffeta gown,
fabric undulating in waves,
camouflaging steps
that were always meant to be taken,
tossing
heelless high heels aside.

EVIL

is a warm tongue on a first date

Evil smells like grass that shouldn't be cut
an over-chlorinated pool

Evil sweats
while sleeping through the day as its pills expire
wakes to be danced
through the night as if it were a demigod

Evil feels like a chain link fence pressing into shoulder blades

Evil bites your bottom lip
leaves you standing at dusk raging and swearing that you won't
    give in
but the craving for it comes on like an orgasm

Evil eats you out when you should be looking for a cure

Evil takes your virginity
with the beat dropping in the song you forgot was playing in the
    background
it honeys sweet tea the morning after
drinks it in front of you

Evil won't break eye contact
says *it's just the way I've always been*
leaving its shirts in your drawer
blaming its confusion and crying
can't deal, can't deal, can't deal

Evil knows it will always exist
that you'll always come back to it
it stares into your feeble will while you imagine it
French kissing new lovers

FOR THE NO RICE, NO SPICE KINDA GUY

The poetry
of his jawline
falls apart
when he opens
his mouth.

POST ONE

Snap

Nothing really happens unless there are pics. I'm taking a selfie of us, sunlight hugging our shoulders, your hand around my waist, my tangerine tank top matching your #glutenfree soft serve. Before I let you know if you look good, I want to make sure the frames of my Ray-Bans are sparkling. I'm hotter behind sunglasses, casually leaning on the pier before the sunshine leaves us for good.

Filter

Black & white is how you would filter us because that's your style, but I'm going to make our picture loud with colour, drown us in my aesthetic, in the moment with #noregrets. We're a #relationshipgoals kinda couple, what they see is what they'll want. Adjust the lighting (it can be better), dial up the glow I got coming off of my cheeks. Focus that Versace logo on your sleeve.

Share

#blessed

like like like like like like like like like like like like like like like like like like like like like like like like like like like like like like like like like like like like like like like like like like like like like like like like like like like like like like like like like like like like like like like like like like like like like like like like like like like like like like like like like like like like like like like like like like like like

13

BOY

Surrounded by white wolves,
I plunge a hand into the alpha's mouth

and rip out its tongue.
The rest scatter in whimpers.

It's not long before I begin to tear at myself
from fear of what I'm becoming,

crawl into the forest to hide
under a blanket of shimmering, silver moths.

NOD AND BE POLITE

Being unnecessarily reminded to say *hi* to grandpa

    Again

Arm unnecessarily grabbed and shoulder slapped

    Again

Hearing nostalgic stories about Vietnam

    Again

Asked when I will get a girlfriend

    Again

Reminding grandpa that I won't ever have one

    Again

Being told how going to Vietnam for a wife is the norm

    Again *here.*

I'm from here.

TALISMAN

after Leah Horlick's "Amulet"

Five years later, I threw it in the trash:
      a ceramic gargoyle that fit
in my palm, white and pink flowers
      painted on its brown body,
gifted to me when you returned
      from the country of cattleya orchids.
Like trying to figure out our bond,
      I never knew what kind of creature
the figurine was modeled after.
      I held on to it since you stayed
around, kept me in mind
      until you lied, throwing me aside.

PLAINLY

one of these days   i will understand

     one of these days   i will understand

       one of these days   i will understand

         one of these days   i will understand

the distances between us

IN THE BACK OF THE SUNFIRE

The rubber is ripped off, tossed
somewhere at your feet. August feels
like it will go on forever
when I bite your bottom lip.

Shifting between wants and needs,
rocking back and forth on top,
I hope to know you by more
than the sweetness of your precum.

But when I catch my breath,
summer slips away
like the sensation of your body
sliding out of mine.

GRANVILLE AND WEST GEORGIA

A stroll through Downtown Vancouver
working out a poem that's been
gestating for weeks. Pigeons congregate,
clucking, pecking at bread crumbs,
bits of plastic around a hot dog stand
by the dilapidated London Drugs.
People weave through the flock
but the birds don't take wing, too preoccupied
with picking up and dropping litter
from their beaks, hopscotching across
dried speckles of their own shit.
I want this poem to have your name in it,
but still keep myself far from memories
of us. I'll write you into a line or two
without becoming the victim
of my own imagination. *Thomas.*
A couple steps forward. *William, Henry.*
There's more pigeon shit under my TOMs
than I realized. *Zachary, Lucas, Eric.*
Every time a new pseudonym
comes to mind—*David*—a bird flies off, searching
for somewhere better before it returns.

2.
BECAUSE
I
AM

STUBBLE BURN

You wait for him over coffee.
It is innocent so long
as you keep adding sugar.
Sorry I'm late. The last
time he apologized, you turned
yourself into an ex. Keep it innocent.
Keep it innocent. Don't stop
adding sugar. Add sugar.
Add sugar. Add sugar.

Your mind wanders to how it felt
to spend time in a room
that has never really left you.
You recall telling him too many
secrets. Before you could lick them all
back from his lips, you notice
the glass of water hasn't fallen
off the nightstand onto the mattress
so maybe it's all going to be worth it.

So you take him in, his tongue
kind between your thighs.
You're so my type is lovely
in the moment because
that's just how romance works.
But when he cums inside,
you want to leave your body.
Water spills onto the mattress.
He drips out of you. Drips. Drips.
Drips.

Doggy-style, doggy-breath. He
compliments *your amazing ass*
in the heat. He helps you
finish with a bite here, here, there.
I'm your rice queen slips
through his teeth and you swallow
salt. If cum splatters can be read
like tealeaves yours are
shaped like black beetles.

Your skin starts to crawl. His
words hit you when he meant
for them to kiss. He kisses
your sweaty brow and moves
down your neck. His stubble
burns in a way you can't stand.
A lump forms in your throat.
To stay calm you focus on un-syncing
your breathing from his.

You feel bigger than the skin
that holds you, which he worships.
Can we still have coffee tomorrow?
You promise yourself that's all
you will have with him from now
on. So long as you keep conversation
innocent, say only what you want,
not what you think he would like. Speak
less sweetly. Less sweet. Less sweet.

POEM MADE FROM KINDLING

What's happening is like a needle
finally finding its sweet spot

entering at the perfect angle so the flow starts,
a steady rush slowing time around two bodies

when it should keep moving
like any other day.

On any other day a kiss would just be a kiss
but this, this is the cure for hoping too long,

as in, only minutes after meeting
asking: how long is too long

to hold a gaze? Maybe on another day
everything could be brushed aside

like the strands in this silver fox's hair,
but his wedding band glimmers

and I'm reminded that I'm being
watched though a framed photo.

NICE TO MEET YOU

this poem is not exotic
this poem is not exotic

these letters are not exotic
these words are not exotic

this poem is not exotic
this poem is not exotic

this mouth is not exotic
this voice is not exotic

this poem is not exotic
this poem is not exotic

BECAUSE I AM

Did he wink at me because I am
because I am and he isn't I wonder if
That boy is a monster
my song is on and
        I move unable to stop obsessing
M-m-m-monster
likes the way I dance because I am
the way my hair is done because I am
likes the way
        I shoot Jägerbombs after a
                blue Lucozade in the alley
because I am
        wondering
if he and I together
would just be an overplayed chorus
He's a wolf
        in disguise
but I can't stop staring in those evil eyes
because I see him preying
        smooth, slim built boys
seemingly submissive
with almond-shaped eyes
        dancing right into his claws
        because now I am because
He ate my heart
        and then he ate my brain
because at times
I am the monster dissecting
what I am

TRANSIT ROMANCE GUY

is denim on denim, denim jeans and a jacket
each morning in the same crowded bus
where the heat's always too high,
a terrarium on wheels again and again at 7 a.m.

Seeds of a romance he doesn't know he's part of
grow when we go our separate ways,
for the rest of the day he's a student of botany
or has recently locked down his LSAT all nonchalant in
   light wash,
poor fingernail hygiene due to construction

from the night before, working 'till 3 a.m.
helping mom because dad walked out a few years ago.
Transit Romance Guy has a good heart
despite the resting bitch face,

which would probably make us
the worst couple in the universe,
two men who look like they don't care for anything.
Transit Romance Guy is a man with complexities,
nuances, a charming obliviousness

to how he moves those around him,
how he moves around in spray-on jeans
through my imagination where I hope he thinks about us,
how we casually nod to each other every morning,

coincidentally see each other again on the bus in the evening.
When the day is over, my mind is tired from running
circles around what to say to him. To him,
the day's just another day
and my face just another face in passing.

Nearing my stop I turn to ask him to pull the cord
but before I say anything, we lock eyes
and everything halts—
his hand lets go and the bus doors open.

WHERE ARE YOU *REALLY* FROM?

Sent to ESL class in fifth grade

      Went home to finish Harry Potter on the loveseat

Told to learn about the Irish potato famine through an early-readers book

      Read about red-eared slider turtles in bed out of curiosity

Failed math tests to everyone's surprise

      Finished spelling tests the quickest

Memories recalled because they cease to mummify

      Ice melts in the champagne bucket while he waits

LOGGING ON

Are we all trying to look for the *right guy on the wrong app*?
What are we supposed to say to the gay who is "just browsing"?

No one knows what a nice dick pic looks like,
but you'll definitely know when you feel dirty seeing one.

As simple as it is, hookup culture is confusing as fuck.
"Oral only" probably has it figured out though,

"We're a Scruff success story <3" is online looking for a third,
and that's cool except they want someone a bit more fem.

Are you going to say hi to your friend when you scroll past them?

Instead of looking for the right guy to get you off (on) the apps,
maybe you just need to find ways to exist as the right you IRL.

Maybe you *are* the kind of guy who can do an open relationship,
and wearing your heart on your sleeve doesn't have to be a fault,
    but a weapon?

MYTHICAL MAN (II)

We press against each other
    so hard
      that I should just admit
I want to be
    absorbed into you,
        our atoms
amalgamating
until we become a hydra
    writhing
  with one hundred hissing
    heads poised
        to strike.
But the harder I try
  to inhabit this idea
the more I know
of its futility—
      eventually, each head
  will be sliced off,
tar-black blood
    kissing the hilt
of my sword.
I'll need to cauterize
        each wound
to prevent
  our dreams
    from regrowing,
distractions
    from the real magic
    that makes us

powerful
on our own.

I FINALLY LEARNED HOW TO LOVE MYSELF

Maybe he thought *sticky rice* was cute
to say after we fucked,
but I was hoping for an experience
where we could exist beyond an expression
that describes two Asians together.
I discovered that everything I despise
about how the world delimits people
infected him so that not even the way
I made him sweat could expel it from his body.
The truth: I took him inside
because I finally learned how to love myself.

CRY

and the devil limps over to you,
bows to be crowned with white orchids
Blink the doubt from your eyes before it blooms
on a black lake in the crater of a planetoid
For what it's worth, learn how to wear
the glow of stars once they burn out
The trick is to know that a safe distance away
from darkness won't help you see better

Instead, rip the sky down, origami-fold it into a beetle
and slip it under your tongue
A star died one billion years ago and tonight you are living
in its afterglow like how a hound leaps
through flames licking at its heels
Bravery is where you worry it might be
Let the devil cry on you

3.
MESSAGE RECEIVED

DISCO THE PUG IS MINE

I haven't adopted him yet,
but he's mine.

Other things can be yours: the lava lamp,
the shake weight,
the room where you write.

But Disco can wander in
whenever he feels like it.

You can't write poems about Disco—just don't.

He won't appreciate your words
concerning his buggy eyes, how
you liken them to the cartoon
that traumatized you

when you were a child.

If the lava lamp spooks him,
then we'll have to donate it. When you use the shake weight

and it agitates Disco

(because it obviously will),
then take a step back
and reconsider
where your priorities are in this relationship.

Your arms aren't getting any bigger.

And, you know,
we'll have to get Disco a stick.
        If we snap your old lacrosse stick, that could work.

Don't give me that,
        you know
I didn't agree to our first date
because you're a great lacrosse player.

        You know I hate sports.

        But Disco needs to run. Needs exercise,
needs to chase something, needs you

        to need me
        and what I need,
                needs you to stop running after

a different version
        of what I'm offering here.

CELEBRITY SIGHTING

Wednesday means I can look at the day
with optimism or pessimism. Not all love
songs in my ear buds have to be about
you. I don't need to think about how today's
air feels humid and still, like the first night
we caught eyes on the SkyTrain.
This cart is empty save for a man
sitting across from me who looks
like a mid-twenties Michael Fassbender,
and a little bit like you, if I'm being honest.
I have a thing for men with sunken cheeks,
an air of unpredictability in their eyes.
He's wearing wireless retro-big, rose
gold headphones, tapping his foot
to a rhythm I'm trying to tap
into but can't follow. It's Wednesday
so it's been two or three weeks
since we last texted. I hope memories
of me haunt you through love songs
that you forgot you had on your phone.
Fassbender's lookalike slips off his cans,
tilts his head up, and our eyes meet
for a beat before he moves to the window
to see if we've reached Granville Station,
the place where you and I parted
and I endured the long thirty minutes
back to my bed. Today, when the SkyTrain
enters and leaves the station,
Fassbender still onboard,
I click on a song that doesn't remind me of you.

MESSAGE RECEIVED

You're cute but I'm not into Asians. Sorry just a preference.

Change your photo. Let the fish
on your arm play peek-a-boo
because a bit of colour entices. Congratulations:
twenty torsos unlock in your area. Five *no azns*
plz. Four variations on *I'm not racist, I just have*
preferences. Six suspected bots, which prove
to be human on your friend's phone. Your total
number of failed conversations through apps reveals
how quiet the world can be to you
or to that closeted Asian boy
daydreaming into the night for rooftop parties
with endless daiquiris when he finally has enough courage
to come out. He sits on the bus on his phone
typing his fourth *hey, what's up?* after deleting eight
other messages that received no responses. How does
he voice himself in this sea of gay men
where so many of us drown in our skin, the ink that covers it?

WHITE+++

Asian
selected
from
drop
down
menu

only
drops
pants
for
tops
seeking
gaysians

POST TWO

Snap

Nothing is real unless our hair is coiffed and we're effortlessly flexing. Seen by my 1,000,000 followers: my BF and I casually leaning against the pier. He hates the smell of the ocean. I ignore the sting of another's cologne on his neck as I lick ice cream from his lips. The lighting is good to us tonight. Makes me look better than him.

Filter

This filter makes us seem like we're together, ideal, a jealousy-invoking adjective. Saturates the nastiness vibrating off us. Softens the bags my eyes gathered from waiting up all night for him to come home. Focuses on the Versace logo on my sleeve, the frame of his Ray-Bans. Erases any evidence that we aren't the type of guys to be each other's type.

Share

#bae and I soaking in the last bit of perfect sunshine before it leaves us for good

like like like like like like like like like like like like like like
like like like like like like like like like like like like like like
like like like like like like like like like like like like like like
like like like like like like like like like like like like like like
like like like like like like like like like like like like like like
like like like like like like like like like like like like like like

ANOTHER MESSAGE RECEIVED

...FORCE THIS WHITE BITCH TO SERVE YR ORIENTAL NOODLE!!!!

All you do is blink, delete
the *no thank you,*
wishing you could escape
your body. But you delete

the app, briefly, re-downloading
discovering you're still
only desired when they lust
for a vacation in your skin,

eager to gorge on yr oriental noodle.

MYTHICAL MAN (III)

This will only feel
like forever for now.
You are not small.
David, you can be good.
You did try. You do try.

SHRINKING DISTANCE

1 kilometre away
In white gay men
In my own preferences
In how I'm not a racist
In a semicolon and right bracket
In a less-than sign and the number three
In straight up racism
In correcting someone's pronunciation of my last name
In not bothering to correct my last name's pronunciation
In a chat that suddenly goes silent
In typing *hey* but fully expecting to be ignored
In the anxiety of approaching men

750 metres away
In faceless profile pics
In the definitions of coffee, friends, and benefits
In movies I don't see myself in
In someone I am mistaken for
In having to ask for a photo
In sharing photos
In blues eyes and warm mouths
In my own skin
In the way he held my neck

350 metres away
In being asked where I'm from
In what they want to know, their inability to know
In temptations to go back to him
In making up futures with him

In the future for queer people of colour
In the way he lays on top of me
In how he lies

150 metres away
In how this is all too real
In how he ignored the *no*
In how I lie for him

50 metres away
In why they say "but I love Asians"
In being buzzed into his building

SKY ZONE TRAMPOLINE PARK

You get off your couch and take an evening off swiping
left, left, right, right, right,
        left to hang out with a friend
at a trampoline park because people don't meet
                        IRL enough anymore.

It's enough to get out of your onesie and put on jeans.

You meet him: he begins bouncing,
                moving with white-guy confidence.
Tell me about the poetry you write?

He asks this while showing that trampolines
                aren't as dangerous as you think.

Maybe his jumps require more focus than they appear to need
so that when you answer, he won't hear "gay stuff."
                You aren't quite sure
if he responds.

Just trust your body to know what to do when going down.
Try it.
        You bounce until your leg muscles coil tight.
                        They spring open, launching you up.
!!!!

You don't hear what he yells; too afraid of not catching
                your balance,
but you do hear that his girlfriend has a fear of trampolines.

Motion sickness starts with regret.
        You lose trust in your body.

                Your bounces are cautious,
    not quite in tandem with his.

GOOD MORNING, BABES

Three in the morning
let's get chicken nuggets,
let's laugh our way
out of The Junction

where the bass
keeps pulsing
in our chests.
Quick, wave that cab—

summer rains,
skinny denim shorts,
damp low-cut tees
plastered to our backs.

Here, paper plates
bleed onto the street,
the rainbow crosswalk
so white at first light.

4.
WILD
SPELL

WAKING AT THE BEGINNING OF THE WORLD

I guess I didn't let go
      when the time before came to an end.

With a single pull,
          you burst from rock,
eras projecting in all directions—
      one sliced my chin, another
         grazed our hands
as they unclasped.

Burgundy eyelashes, a smile,
      and you grabbed my wrist,
bolted for dunes
that rolled on and on—I swear
      every step made the desert
seem more vast.

      There, a serpent stopped us
as it burst from the sand,
bulbous black head
staring us down,
      flicking its leathery tongue,
opening its mouth and inviting us inside.

With your free hand,
      you calmly stroked one of its fangs.
I shuddered
when it simultaneously snapped its jaws shut,
      dove

back into the sand,
shifting sparkling grains on the surface
as it swerved beneath.

You let go of me, broke
into a chase after it. I followed.

Now, we run towards the beasts.

NYMPHAEACEAE

I should have believed more as a boy.
If I were to pass myself now in a dream,
    I wouldn't feel guilty
            for moments of self compassion.
                They bloom
  in the imagination like pink lilies
bobbing on a boiling black lake.

    I'd tell myself that I'm just a bud
    of tangled magic,
            a page from a childhood grimoire
       crumpled and thrown into a fire
because I couldn't find the spell I was looking for fast enough.

    Boy, magic exists—
count one two three,
    welcome the tingling underneath your skin
       and sit with how uncomfortable it can become.

ALMOST, BUT NOT QUITE

After I swallow
a bit of iced tea, I place the glass
back on to the wet ring
it leaves on the table between us.

—

You clear your throat
with a grumble
I first hated, but grew to adore
when I'd wake up next to you.

—

I'm sorry,
you must feel really shitty—
an apology absent
of everything I need to hear.

—

What to expect
from someone who keeps
missing their coaster
by mere millimetres?

MYTHICAL MAN (IV)

Echoing my ancestors,
my hands rattle
every reachable, rusted lock
beyond belonging,
beyond what is understood,
what can be created or destroyed.

HUNT

Have you noticed how sharp and sparkly
your talons are in the starlight?
Let me lick them clean once you've finished
stirring up my sweetest and most tender parts.
Pupils dilated, I see hunters
who've been stalking this forest for you
the moment you entered to seek me out.
Clutch me in the dark—together we'll stay
silent as I brush the vertebrae
protruding from your charcoal-flecked skin.

WILD SPELL

after Kai Cheng Thom's "peat moss man"

A man made from parts of the dead.
Bones blessed with viper venom,
a rib cage that won't crack
as he expands to swallow
the entire world. A man dressed
in cuttlefish chromatophores
for when he wants to hide,
wants others to see him, for when
he only wants to be seen by me.
Gastropod shells are ground down
to a fine powder and dusted
over his pink lips—he won't be able
to help but to slowly kiss
incantations along my neck.
Soon, his nectar bat tongue
slips from my body's sweetest parts,
his hands sporting
talons to clutch someone else
who can better love the wildness
that wished him into existence.

I JUST WANTED A BLUE HAWAIIAN

Lady Gaga gives a million reasons
to dance closer to the emptiness
but I stay at the bar half-shouting
            to the lip-syncing bartender
to get his attention. I want
        a Blue Hawaiian to replace
        my shattered Long Island Iced Tea.

A hand cut from marble
reaches past me to pay for my drink. I turn, putting
tongue to teeth, but he winks
        before *thank you* slips from my lips.
His monster jawline and cerulean-eyed kindness
makes me wonder if he did it because
        he wants to know me
or knows there are millions of me.

STATE OF MAN

With a stone loaded
    in my slingshot,
        I pull
    back
    taut
and aim at the chest
of a statue I chiseled
in his likeliness,
    petrified,
        deceptively gentle,
the softness in his brow
welcoming me,
his open arms enticing me
    to safety.
When I release,
    launching the stone
        that shatters him
        into a cloud
    of marbled dust,
    he clears the way for me
to walk in a world
that is better grounded
in reality,
    not constructed
      on a foundation
        that equates my worth
    with how I worship.

FINALLY

The salt on your cheeks
needs to be wiped away. To be honest,
the devil should not be remembered
only when he wants to be.

He's there when you slip, lacerating
the bottoms of your toes
on barnacles, and he's there
when you slurp back ice-cold oysters

on the shoreline, golden and hot
with citrus
running down your stubbled chin,
speckling the sand's darkness.

Before you leave, be sure to stand
and limp over if you have to.
Find where the devil stands
in the water, a wading merman

from the waist up. He'll bow,
patient and understanding,
forgiving and waiting
to kiss the tears from your cheeks.

WALKING TOGETHER AT THE END OF THE WORLD

and calling you mine will be like naming
the cosmic phenomenon no one thought to look for

in Scorpius, a burst of bronze
light at the tip of its stinger that sparked

the reversal of poles scientists had anticipated
for so long. We traverse hand-in-hand

across frozen seas, across engulfed metropoles
built to withstand the apocalypse, the ice

beneath our feet pulsating with the glow
of a skyscraper-sized cuttlefish.

Rubbing my eyes, a frozen black eyelash
sits in my palm. You insist that I make a wish

before we move on, but just as I'm about to
mutter the words, a breeze lifts the eyelash

from my skin and it dances through the air,
lengthens into a tendril that splits

into writhing tentacles that lash my frost-bitten face.
To what end are you imagining, David?

NOTES

The lyrics used in "Because I Am" are from Lady Gaga's song "Monster" on her extended play, *The Fame Monster* (2009), a reissue of her debut studio album, *The Fame* (2008).

The quotes in "Message Received" and "Another Message Received" are taken from messages received on the online dating app Grindr.

ACKNOWLEDGMENTS

"Celebrity Sighting" can be read in *The /tɛmz/ Review*'s Winter 2018 issue, while "Transit Romance Guy" and "Walking Together at the End of the World" appear in the Winter 2019 issue, all with slight changes.

Pulp Literature published an early version of "Cry" in issue 22.

The Puritan published an early version of "Because I Am" in issue 37.

"White+++" appeared in *PRISM international*, issue 56.3 "Bad."

"Logging On" appeared in *This Magazine*'s Summer 2019 issue.

The following poems were published in the chapbook *Stubble Burn* (Anstruther Press, 2018), with changes: "Another Message Received," "Because I Am," "For the No Rice, No Spice Kinda Guy," "Message Received," "Post Two," "Stubble Burn" and "White+++".

"Transit Romance Guy" and "Cry" were nominated for a 2019 Pushcart Prize.

A previous iteration of "Message Received" was long-listed for the 2017 Thomas Morton Memorial Prize in Literary Excellence.

THANK YOU

To Jim Johnstone, editor extraordinaire and friend, for first welcoming *Stubble Burn* to the Anstruther family. Thank you for seeing the magic in my poetry (and in me) when I have difficulty seeing it myself.

To Kate Hargreaves for creating the lovely snakeskin look for this book. Thank you so much.

To Aimée Parent Dunn and everyone else at Palimpsest for your work, passion, and dedication.

To Daniel Zomparelli for writing *Davie St. Translations,* and reading my baby poems so long ago. Dina Del Bucchia, thank you for being an absolute freaken delight.

To Kai Cheng Thom, Jen Sookfong Lee, Vivek Shraya, Ben Rawluk, Adèle Barclay, Leah Horlick, and Amber Dawn for inspiring bravery.

To David Chariandy, Anosh Irani, Broc Rossell, and Cecily Nicholson, teachers who kindly nurtured my craft.

To the Canada Council of the Arts for funding that sustained me while writing.

To all of the magazines that have published my poems.

And to you, reader, for greeting *Mythical Man* with an open heart.

DAVID LY is the author of the chapbook *Stubble Burn* (2018) and *Mythical Man* is his first full-length collection. His poetry has appeared in an array of publications such as *PRISM international, carte blanche, The Maynard, Pulp Literature,* and *The /tɛmz/ Review.* David has also been nominated for a Pushcart Prize, and he has been long- and short-listed for the Thomas Morton Memorial Prize in Literary Excellence and the Magpie Award for Poetry, respectively. Twitter: @dlylyly.